What DO YOU THINK?

SHOULD ANIMALS LIVE IN ZOOS?

BY RAYMIE DAVIS

Gareth Stevens
PUBLISHING

Please visit our website, www.garethstevens.com. For a free color catalog of all our high-quality books, call toll free 1-800-542-2595 or fax 1-877-542-2596.

Library of Congress Cataloging-in-Publication Data
Names: Davis, Raymie, author.
Title: Should animals live in zoos? / by Raymie Davis.
Description: New York : Gareth Stevens Publishing, [2023] | Series: What do you think? | Includes index. | Audience: Grades 2-3
Identifiers: LCCN 2021044972 (print) | LCCN 2021044973 (ebook) | ISBN 9781538278673 (paperback) | ISBN 9781538278697 (library binding) | ISBN 9781538278680 (set) | ISBN 9781538278703 (ebook)
Subjects: LCSH: Captive wild animals–Juvenile literature. | Zoo animals–Juvenile literature. | Animal rights–Juvenile literature.
Classification: LCC HV4708 .D365 2023 (print) | LCC HV4708 (ebook) | DDC 179/.3–dc23
LC record available at https://lccn.loc.gov/2021044972
LC ebook record available at https://lccn.loc.gov/2021044973

First Edition

Portions of this work were originally authored by Nick Christopher and published as *Should We Keep Animals in Zoos?* All new material this edition authored by Raymie Davis.

Published in 2023 by
Gareth Stevens Publishing
29 East 21st Street
New York, NY 10010

Copyright © 2023 Gareth Stevens Publishing

Editor: Caitie McAneney
Designer: Michael Flynn

Photo credits: Cover, p. 1 Vadim Gorbenko/Shutterstock.com; back cover and series background MYMNY/Shutterstock.com; p. 5 mikeledray/Shutterstock.com; p. 7 Inna Tolstorebrova/Shutterstock.com; p. 8 belizar/Shutterstock.com; p. 9 Philip Lange/Shutterstock.com; p. 10 Razmarinka/Shutterstock.com; p. 11 Ilina Yuliia/Shutterstock.com; p. 13 RPBaiao/Shutterstock.com; p. 15 Peter Betts/Shutterstock.com; p. 16 mikumistock/Shutterstock.com; p. 17 FamVeld/Shutterstock.com; p. 19 Valentina/Shutterstock.com; p. 21 Hugo Brizard - YouGoPhoto/Shutterstock.com.

All rights reserved. No part of this book may be reproduced in any form without permission in writing from the publisher, except by a reviewer.

Printed in the United States of America

Some of the images in this book illustrate individuals who are models. The depictions do not imply actual situations or events.

CPSIA compliance information: Batch #CSGS23: For further information contact Gareth Stevens, New York, New York at 1-800-542-2595.

CONTENTS

Zoo Animals 4

What Are Animal Rights? 6

Providing Care 8

Animals Suffering 10

Endangered Species 12

Not Natural 14

It's Educational! 16

Not For Learning 18

What's More Important? 20

Glossary 22

For More Information 23

Index 24

WORDS IN THE GLOSSARY APPEAR IN **BOLD** TYPE THE FIRST TIME THEY ARE USED IN THE TEXT.

ZOO ANIMALS

Have you ever been to a zoo? Children often go to zoo with their families, friends, or schools. They are important in many communities. People go there to see and learn about animals. But some people believe zoos aren't good for animals. They think wild animals should only live in the wild.

What do you think? It's helpful to understand why people on both sides of this **debate** feel the way they do. After you learn the arguments and facts, you can make an informed opinion.

WHAT ARE ANIMAL RIGHTS?

Zoos are nothing new. People have kept wild animals in **captivity** for a long time. Before zoos, rich people kept collections of wild animals to show off their wealth and power. The word "zoo" was first used to describe London's zoological gardens in the 1800s.

Over time, people began speaking out about the practice of keeping wild animals in zoos. Groups such as People for the Ethical Treatment of Animals (PETA) fight for animal **welfare**. Animal rights groups made people think about if zoos might be harmful to wild animals.

Think ABOUT IT!

THE FIRST MODERN ZOOS WERE BUILT IN EUROPE IN THE 1700S.

ANIMAL RIGHTS GROUPS RAISE AWARENESS ABOUT HOW ZOOS TREAT THEIR ANIMALS.

PROVIDING CARE

Some people say that zoos are helpful to animals because they provide care. In many zoos, animals are fed a healthy diet, or food. In the wild, they might not be able to get enough food or the right food. Also, zoos have **veterinarians** who provide medical care for hurt or sick animals. Those animals would often be left to die in the wild.

Zoos help smaller animals that are hunted by larger animals in the wild. They help animals who suffer from **habitat** loss in the wild, such as panda bears.

Think About IT!

IN SOME CASES, ZOOS HELP ANIMALS LIVE LONGER. A 2016 STUDY SHOWED THAT MOST **MAMMALS** LIVE LONGER IN ZOOS THAN THEY DO IN THE WILD.

MOST ZOOKEEPERS LOVE THEIR ANIMALS. THEY GIVE ANIMALS TOYS AND EXERCISES TO HELP THEM LEARN AND PLAY.

ANIMALS SUFFERING

Other people argue that zoos don't make every kind of animal live longer. Some larger mammals live longer in the wild. Elephants live nearly twice as long in the wild as they do in captivity.

The mental health of zoo animals is an area of growing concern. "Zoochosis" is the word commonly used for the strange actions and mental problems that an animal displays because it's in captivity. A number of zoo animals suffer from **depression** and **anxiety**. People say it isn't fair to keep them caged and **stressed**.

ENDANGERED SPECIES

Endangered **species** are animals that are in danger of dying out. Zoos can save these species. People argue that zoos are important to **conservation** efforts. **Breeding** programs in zoos around the world aim to increase the populations of endangered species. In most cases, the plan is to let those animals go back into the wild.

The Association of Zoos and Aquariums (AZA) is the leader in caring for endangered species. It leads conservation programs to help species such as the California condor and American red wolf.

Think ABOUT IT!

GOLDEN LION TAMARIN MONKEYS ALMOST DIED OUT FROM HABITAT LOSS IN BRAZIL. BREEDING PROGRAMS IN ZOOS AROUND THE WORLD RAISED THE WILD POPULATION TO 3,500.

ENDANGERED ANIMALS SAVED BY ZOOS

- CALIFORNIA CONDOR
- BLACK-FOOTED FERRET
- AMERICAN RED WOLF
- GOLDEN LION TAMARIN
- PRZEWALSKI'S HORSE

THIS 130-YEAR-OLD TORTOISE WAS TAKEN FROM THE GALÁPAGOS ISLANDS TO THE SAN DIEGO ZOO, WHERE IT BECAME THE FATHER OF HUNDREDS OF TORTOISES TO SAVE THE SPECIES.

NOT NATURAL

While some people think zoos help save endangered species, other people argue that zoos aren't a normal habitat. Life in a zoo is very different from life in an animal's natural habitat. Zoo animals don't learn hunting skills since they're fed by zookeepers. They also don't learn to stay away from predators in captivity.

Zoo animals also don't learn to fear people. This leads to them being hit by cars or shot by hunters in the wild. Some argue it's unfair to release zoo animals into the wild without the right skills or knowledge.

ANIMALS THAT LIVE IN ZOOS DON'T LEARN THE SKILLS THEY WOULD IN THE WILD, SUCH AS HUNTING.

IT'S EDUCATIONAL!

Many people believe zoos are helpful because they educate people about animals. When children visit zoos, it often sparks a lifelong love for animals. They get to see wild animals they would never see otherwise in a safe setting. This helps them form a deeper connection with nature.

Zoos show children that they share Earth with wild animals and that they must help care for endangered species and other creatures. Then they might be interested in conservation efforts for the rest of their life.

MILLIONS OF STUDENTS VISIT ZOOS EACH YEAR ON FIELD TRIPS TO LEARN ABOUT ANIMALS.

NOT FOR LEARNING

Some people argue that kids aren't learning anything at the zoo, or they're not learning the right lessons. It's not easy for children to learn how animals act in the wild when they visit a zoo.

Groups such as PETA believe zoos teach children that it's fine to keep animals in cages instead of in the wild. Some people also worry that zoos make the public care less about conservation. These people might think they don't have to help endangered animals because zoos seem to be doing the work.

Think ABOUT IT!

A 2014 STUDY OF VISITORS TO THE LONDON ZOO SHOWED THAT MORE THAN 60% OF CHILDREN DIDN'T GAIN ANY NEW KNOWLEDGE OF ANIMALS FROM THEIR VISIT.

ANIMALS AREN'T USED TO LIVING IN CAGES, SO WHAT YOU SEE AT ZOOS ISN'T HOW THEY WOULD NORMALLY ACT.

WHAT'S MORE IMPORTANT?

Some people think zoos keep animals safe and educate people about conservation. Other people think that animals deserve their freedom. Both sides care a lot about the topic.

In recent years, people who run zoos have worked hard to build habitats that are more like the places animals live in the wild. That's one way that debate can help make positive change. You've heard the arguments on both sides. What do you think about this important debate?

SOME PEOPLE SAY THAT IT DOESN'T MATTER HOW WELL A ZOO BUILDS A HABITAT—IT'S STILL NOT NATURAL.

GLOSSARY

anxiety: fear or nervousness

breed: to produce young

captivity: the state of being kept in a place and unable to escape

conservation: the careful management of the natural world

debate: an argument or discussion about an issue, generally between two sides

depression: a mental disorder marked by sadness and a lack of interest in doing anything

habitat: the natural place where an animal or plant lives

mammal: any warm-blooded animal that has babies that drink milk and a body covered with hair or fur

species: a group of plants or animals that are all of the same kind

stressed: made to feel mental pressure

veterinarian: a doctor who is trained to treat animals

welfare: the state of doing well

FOR MORE INFORMATION

BOOKS

DiSpezio, Michael A. *Animal Atlas for Kids: A Visual Journey of Wildlife from Around the World.* Emeryville, CA: Rockridge Press, 2021.

Ganeri, Anita. *Endangered Animals.* New York City, NY: Rosen Publishing, 2018.

Regan, Lisa. *Planet Earth: Habitats.* New York City, NY: Rosen Publishing, 2020.

WEBSITES

Ducksters: Zoos
www.ducksters.com/animals/zoos.php
Learn more about zoos and how they can help animals.

San Diego Zoo Kids
kids.sandiegozoowildlifealliance.org/
Explore exciting facts about animals with the San Diego Zoo!

U.S. Fish and Wildlife Service: California Condor
www.fws.gov/sacramento/es_kids/CA-Condor/
Discover the story of how zoos helped save the California condor.

Publisher's note to educators and parents: Our editors have carefully reviewed these websites to ensure that they are suitable for students. Many websites change frequently, however, and we cannot guarantee that a site's future contents will continue to meet our high standards of quality and educational value. Be advised that students should be closely supervised whenever they access the internet.

INDEX

Association of Zoos and Aquariums (AZA) 12

animal rights groups 6, 7

animal welfare 6

captivity 6, 10, 14

communities 4

conservation 12, 16, 18, 20

elephants 10, 11

endangered species 12, 13, 14, 16, 18

hunting 14, 15

learning 4, 9, 14, 15, 16, 17, 18

mental health 10

panda bears 8

People for the Ethical Treatment of Animals (PETA) 6, 18

San Diego Zoo 5, 13

schools 4

veterinarians 8